Oxford Discover

2nd edition

Writing & Spelling 5

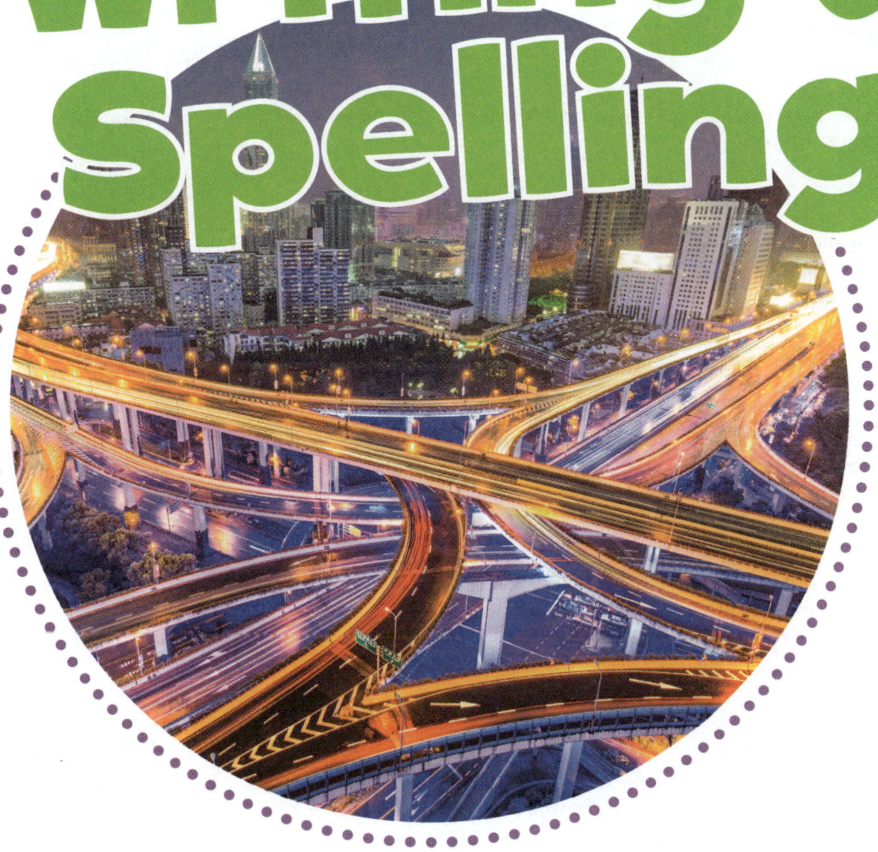

Barbara Mackay

Victoria Tebbs

OXFORD

UNIVERSITY PRESS

Contents

Writing

MODULE	USEFUL WORDS	WRITING FOCUS	WRITING OUTPUT	PLANNING TOOLS
1 Write an emotional appeal for a cause Page 4	vital survey breeding survival funds destruction precious rare fragile needless slaughter vulnerable essential	Emotive language *clean → pure*	Emotional appeal	Planning chart
2 Write about animal senses Page 10	snout beak smell tool nostrils blowhole otter beaver trunk signal	Language of comparison and contrast *similarly, like while, however*	Informational text	Venn diagram Planning chart
3 Write about a process that uses wheels Page 16	turbine industry blade axle mill dammed sluice rotate force transmit gears belts	Ordering: cause and effect *first, this causes, which in turn*	Process text	Sequencing chart
4 Write an interview with an animal Page 22	field stable hay trot pole plod behave express threaten	Adverbs of manner *rudely, delicately*	Interview	Sequencing chart
5 Write about where things come from in the world Page 28	export resource gasoline copper palladium quartz cultural foreign	Topic, supporting, and concluding sentences	Informational text	Paragraph map Notes
6 Write a descriptive text Page 34	leaping jagged stone skylark hover echo laughter skim tempting valley	Personification *The smiling mountain stretched high into the sky …*	Descriptive text	*Wh-* chart
7 Write about a hypothetical situation Page 40	barter trade goods basket labor exchange value skill society	Conditional tenses *What would it be like if … ?*	Hypothetical text	Paragraph map
8 Write an engaging story Page 46	ahead ancient peeling massive rusty handle twitch froze pause dart save	Enriching language *He scrambled frantically over the wall …*	Engaging story	Notes Story map
9 Write about how a building is made Page 52	straw bale foundations timber constructed layer stacked overlapping stake thatch rendered plaster	Passive voice to describe a process *First, the foundations are laid …*	Process report	Sequence chart Notes

Error Correction Master Class Page 58 — How to find and correct: spelling mistakes, punctuation mistakes, verb mistakes, missing words, extra words, wrong words, wrong word order, where a new paragraph should start.
Practice correcting a text using error codes.

Spelling Master Class

MODULE	SPELLING FOCUS AND STRATEGY
1 Page 60	Suffixes *-ible, -able, -ibly, -ably* flexi*ble* predict*able* flex*ibly* predict*ably*
2 Page 61	Prefix *un-* *un*tie *un*happy
3 Page 62	Prefixes *pre-* and *pro-* *pre*view *pro*cess
4 Page 63	Spelling with *ie* and *ei* n*ie*ce rec*ei*ve
5 Page 64	Homophones *by* *buy* *one* *won*
6 Page 65	Mnemonics *u always follows q.*
7 Page 66	Prefixes *in-* and *im-* *in*accurate *im*polite
8 Page 67	Suffixes *-ous* and *-ious* danger*ous* grac*ious*
9 Page 68	Keep a Spelling Log
Wordlist Page 69	Add translations or explanations to help you remember useful words from each module.

Write an emotional appeal for a cause

Read

A An appeal uses emotional language to make the reader respond to a text. What kind of emotional appeals can you think of? Now read the webpage. What is it asking you to do?

Turtle Island Conservation Program in Costa Rica

Turtle Island volunteers are doing vital work to survey Costa Rica's rapidly diminishing turtle population. This valuable information is used to find out how climate change and population expansion are negatively affecting the turtle population.

We need your help!
Our conservation program needs donations in order to:

- monitor breeding patterns
- help the survival of eggs and baby hatchlings
- assess how climate change and population growth is damaging the turtles' habitats

You can make a real difference!
We rely entirely on donations, so we need your help to provide funds for this essential work:

- **$250** will buy a radio for beach communication
- **$650** will train a field assistant
- **$700** will pay a beach guard for a month

Please support this incredible project and help prevent the destruction of Costa Rica's precious turtle population. With your assistance, we can help protect this rare and valuable species, and preserve the beauty of its fragile habitats.

Mission:

- to prevent the poaching of turtle eggs in the breeding season
- to prevent the needless slaughter of turtles for meat
- to help vulnerable hatchlings get to the sea
- to provide education in the local community
- to help preserve the fragile habitats which are essential for the turtles' survival

Understand

B Circle up to five words you don't know from the text in **A**.
Check them with your teacher.

C This appeal has three sections. Number them in the correct order.

- ◯ The funds that they need
- ◯ Their mission
- ◯ What they do

D Which section do you think is the most important part of the appeal? Why?

_____

_____

E Look at these sentences from the "Mission" section. How do the words in bold make you feel?

1 to prevent the **needless slaughter** of turtles for meat

_____

2 to help **vulnerable** hatchlings get to the sea

_____

3 to help preserve **fragile** habitats which are **essential** for the turtles' **survival**

_____

F Complete this emotional appeal with some of these words or your own words.

> fragile   unusual   precious   rare   generations
> vulnerable   vital   ~~destruction~~   terrible

You can help prevent the ___destruction___ of Borneo's _____ rainforest and its _____ orangutans. With your assistance, we can help protect this _____ species and preserve the beauty of its _____ habitats for future _____. Please support this _____ project.

Think

G Think of causes that you would like to support. Make a list.

_____

_____

H Think about your answer to **G**. Choose one cause and ask yourself these questions. Do you know or can you find out:

1 ☐ what the organization does?

2 ☐ why they need funds?

3 ☐ what your donations would buy?

4 ☐ what their mission is?

I Think about your own emotional appeal. Write notes about this cause in the space below.

_____

_____

_____

_____

_____

J 🔍 **Writing Focus**   Emotive Language

Emotive language is chosen by the writer to make the reader feel a certain emotion. Adverbs, adjectives, and nouns can be used to add emotional impact:

killing → slaughter

clean → pure

no money → poverty

valuable → precious

not guilty → innocent

want → need

no food → hunger

loss → destruction

Think of some words you can use to add impact to your emotional appeal.

_____

_____

_____

Organize and Plan

K Think about the sections of the appeal in **A** and create the outline of your emotional appeal.

> **1** Outline what your organization does.
>
> _____
>
> _____
>
> _____
>
> _____

> **2** Explain three things that need funding and how much money is needed.
>
> _____
>
> _____
>
> _____

> **3** Give four bullet points stating the mission.
>
> _____
>
> _____
>
> _____
>
> _____

L What emotion do you want your readers to feel when they read your appeal?

_____

_____

M What photo could you use with your emotional appeal? Describe what it could show and why.

_____

_____

_____

_____

Write Your First Draft

N Now write your emotional appeal. Use your work in activities **H** – **M** to help you. Find and glue a picture.

What the organization does

_____
_____
_____
_____
_____
_____
_____
_____

The funds that they need

_____
_____
_____
_____
_____
_____

Their mission

_____
_____
_____
_____
_____
_____

Edit

O Give your emotional appeal to a partner to check.

 Check your partner's spelling. Circle mistakes and write "**S**" in the margin of page 8.

 Check your partner's writing – are there any missing words? Circle mistakes and write "**M**" in the margin of page 8.

 Check your partner's word order – make sure that nouns come after adjectives. Circle mistakes and write "**WO**" in the margin of page 8.

P Read and check (✓) or cross (✗).

☐ Did your partner write the background to their appeal?

☐ Did your partner explain what funds their appeal needs?

☐ Did your partner write the mission?

☐ Did your partner use emotive language?

Write Your Final Draft

Q Correct your mistakes and type your appeal on a computer. Add a picture. Display your appeals in the classroom. Read them and vote for the most powerful appeal.

Write about animal senses

Read

A An informational text tells the reader about the world. What sort of informational texts can you think of? Now read. Which paragraph in the text did you find most interesting?

How do animals use their noses?

Not all animals have noses. Some animals have snouts or beaks. Most animals use their noses for breathing and smelling, and some use them as a tool.

Many animals have a strong sense of smell. Dogs can smell 1,000 to 10,000 times better than a person. Similarly, a bear's sense of smell is unusually strong. A bear can detect a dead animal 20 miles away. Although not all animals have noses, all animals have a sense of smell. Fish don't have noses, but they have nostrils which they use to smell. A shark can smell a drop of blood in 100 litres of water.

Like fish, whales don't have noses. They have a blowhole which is like a nostril. However, a whale's blowhole isn't used for smelling. It's used for breathing. In the same way that a whale closes its blowhole when it dives, otters and beavers close their nostrils in the water. Similarly, camels close their nostrils to keep out sand. Nostrils help many animals control their breathing.

Some animals use their noses as tools. Anteaters use their snouts to find food in anthills. Similarly, elephants use their trunks to pick up grass or suck up water. In contrast to the anteater, elephants also use their trunks to make a loud noise when they are feeling unsafe or to signal danger.

So, although all animals use their noses for breathing and smelling, others also use them as tools or for making a noise.

Understand

B   Circle up to five words you don't know from the text in **A**.
Check them with your teacher.

C   Look at these sentences from the text in **A**. Are they comparing or contrasting information? Write *compare* or *contrast* for each sentence.

1   Like fish, whales don't have noses. _____

2   However, a whale's blowhole isn't used for smelling. _____

3   Similarly, camels close their nostrils to keep out sand. _____

D   Look at the text in **A** and complete the sentences.

1   Dogs, bears, and _____ have a strong sense of smell.

2   Whales, otters, and _____ can close their nostrils in water
to control their breathing.

3   Anteaters and _____ use their noses as tools.

E   Read this paragraph and look at the diagram. Can you compare and contrast the animals? Write things about them, using the correct question number.

Birds breathe through nostrils in their beaks. They smell through their nostrils. Snakes breathe through their nostrils. They smell with their tongues. Insects "breathe" through holes along their bodies called spiracles. They don't have nostrils like snakes and birds. They detect smells with the antennae on their heads.

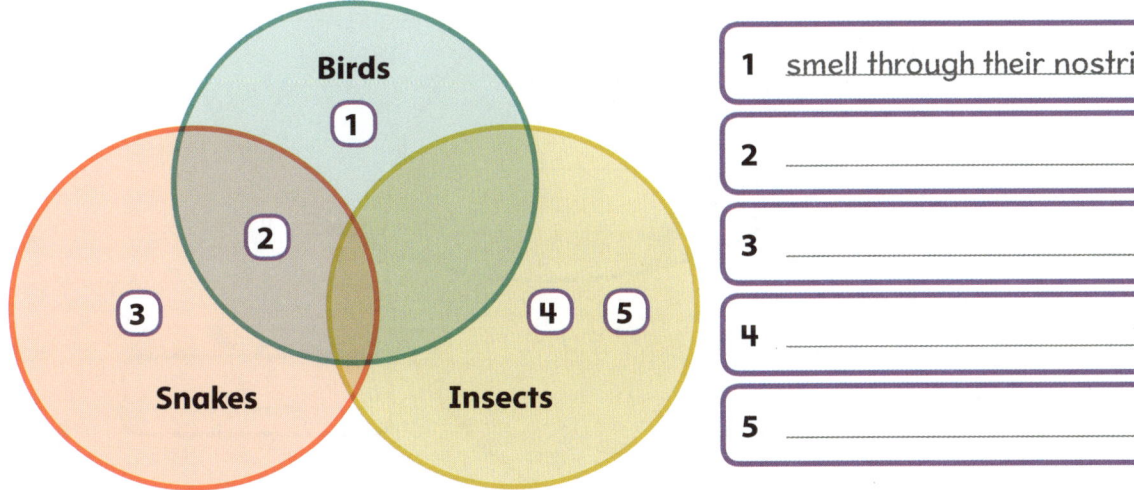

1   smell through their nostrils

2   _____

3   _____

4   _____

5   _____

Think

F Think about different animals or insects, and their ears. What information do you know? Make notes.

_____

_____

_____

_____

G Think about your answer to **F**. Ask yourself these questions.
Do you know or can you find out:

1 ⬜ how the animals hear?

2 ⬜ where their ears are?

3 ⬜ similarities and differences between the animals or insects?

H Choose three animals. Write their names in the purple boxes. Then compare and contrast them, using your information from **G**. Write your answers in the correct part of the diagram.

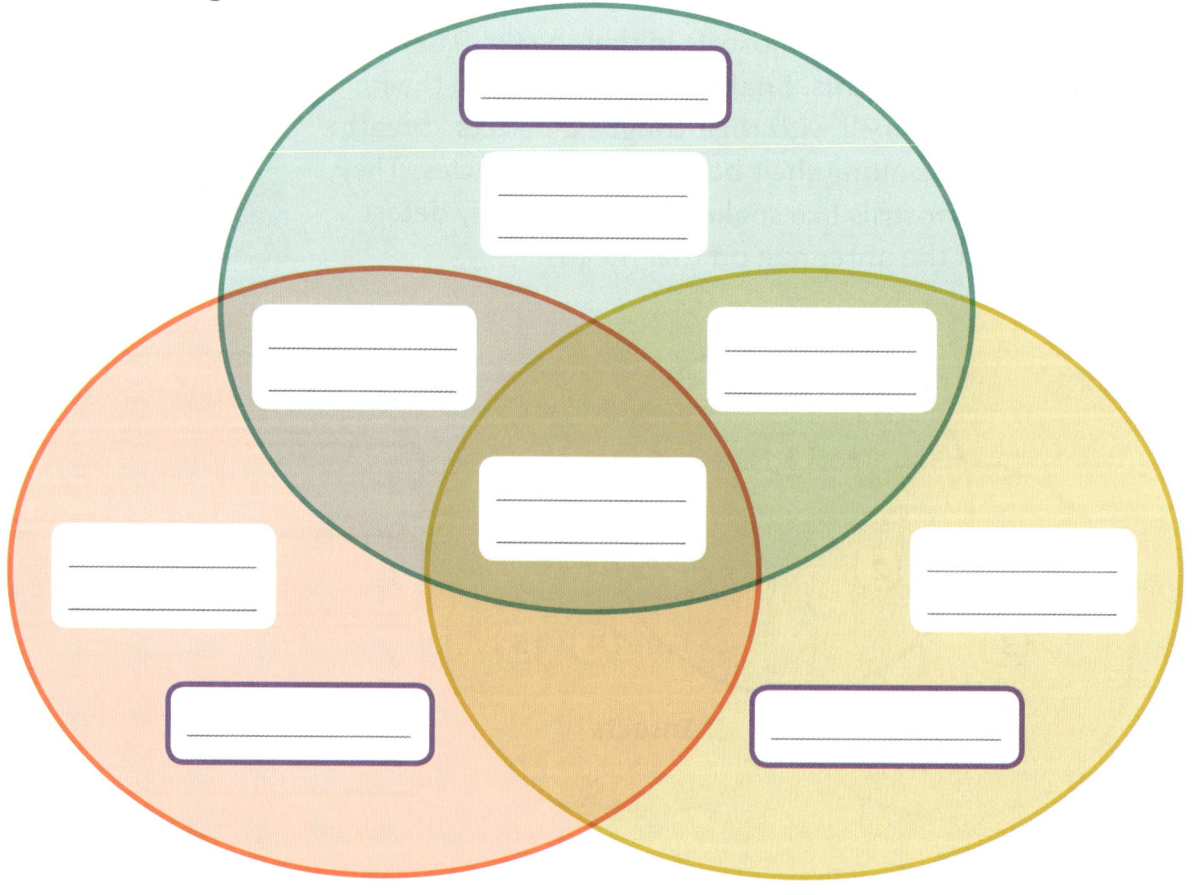

Organize and Plan

I The informational text in **A** can be divided into five paragraphs.
Use your ideas from **H** to make notes for each paragraph in your text.

1 Introduction _____

2 Animals and their sense of hearing _____
_____

3 Ways animals hear using ears _____
_____

4 Position of ears _____
_____

5 Conclusion _____

J 🔍 **Writing Focus** **Language of Comparison and Contrast**

In your writing, you can **compare** things that are the same, and **contrast** things that are different.

Language of comparison
similarly   like   in the same way   also   as well as   and

Language of contrast
while   however   in contrast to   although   but

**Think of ways you can use language to compare and contrast your ideas in
paragraphs 2, 3, and 4. Choose words from the Writing Focus box to help you.**

Animals and their sense of hearing

_____

Ways animals hear using ears

_____

Position of ears

_____

Write Your First Draft

K Now write your informational text. Use your work in activities **F** – **J** to help you. Draw or glue a picture.

Title

Introduction

_____

_____

_____

_____

Paragraph 2

_____

_____

_____

_____

Paragraph 3

_____

_____

_____

_____

Paragraph 4

_____

_____

_____

Conclusion

_____

_____

_____

_____

Edit

L Give your informational text to a partner to check.

 Check your partner's simple present verbs. Circle mistakes and write "**V**" in the margin of page 14.

 Check your partner's writing – is it separated into paragraphs? Circle where a new paragraph should start and write "**[**" in the margin of page 14.

 Check your partner's language of comparison and contrast. Circle mistakes and write "**WW**" in the margin of page 14.

M Read and check (✓) or cross (✗).

☐ Does your partner's informational text have an introduction and a conclusion?

☐ Did your partner compare and contrast different things?

☐ Did your partner use language to compare and contrast in their paragraphs 2, 3, and 4?

Write Your Final Draft

N Correct your mistakes and write your text again in your notebook. Draw or glue a picture. Work in pairs. Read out your texts. Then talk about the most interesting differences between the animals.

Similarly, … However, … In the same way, …

3 Write about a process that uses wheels

Read

A A process text tells the reader how something works. What process texts can you think of? Now read. What is the purpose of a water wheel?

How a water wheel works

Until recently, the water wheel and the water turbine played an important part in industry as a way of changing energy into power. A water wheel is made of a large wheel with a number of blades arranged on the outside of the wheel.

The wheel is attached vertically to a horizontal axle. The wheel must be near a water supply, so that it can use the water to turn it. The water supply may come from a flowing stream, or a mill pond where the stream is dammed.

The process starts with the sluice gate – this is a barrier which controls the flow of water.

First, the sluice gate is opened. This causes the water from the mill pond to rush down a channel called a mill race toward the water wheel. The wheel starts to rotate because the weight of the water pushes against it and turns it around. This creates a force which powers the turbine. The power is transmitted from the turbine through the axle to drive gears or belts. This power can be used for a variety of purposes. In the 19th and early 20th centuries these included grinding flour, hammering iron, making cloth, and crushing wood into pulp to make paper.

Understand

B Circle up to five words you don't know from the text in **A**.
Check them with your teacher.

C Number these sentences in the correct order. Then look at the process text
in **A** and check your answers.

☐ This creates a force which powers the turbine.

☐ This causes the water from the mill pond to rush down a channel
called a mill race toward the water wheel.

☐ The wheel starts to rotate because the weight of the water pushes
against it and turns it around.

☐ First, the sluice gate is opened.

☐ The power is transmitted from the turbine through the axle to drive
gears or belts.

D In order to understand how the water wheel works, we need to understand some
causes and effects.

Cause	Effect
The sluice gate is opened	⇨ and the water rushes down the mill race.
The water pushes against the wheel	⇨ and it rotates.
Power is transmitted through the turbine	⇨ and gears and belts turn.

Ask questions with *Why* and give answers with *Because*.

Why does the water rush down the mill race?	⇨ Because the sluice gate is opened.

_____

_____

_____

_____

Think

E Think of different processes that use wheels. Write your ideas below.

_____

_____

_____

F Think about your answer to **E**. Choose one of your ideas. Ask yourself these questions. Do you know or can you find out:

1 ⬭ how the process works?

2 ⬭ the language you need to explain the process?

G Make notes about your process.

_____

_____

_____

_____

H 🔍 **Writing Focus** **Ordering: Cause and Effect**

When you are writing a process text, you need to explain what **causes** each action, and what **effect** each action has.

Use words which describe the sequence of events:

first   this causes   this makes   which in turn   then   so that

Look at the words in the Writing Focus box which describe the sequence of events. Write these words in the correct place in the chart. Then think about how you can use these sequence words to explain your process.

Cause	Effect

Organize and Plan

I Your process text needs the following structure. Complete the section below with notes about your process. Remember to use sequence words to describe the order of events.

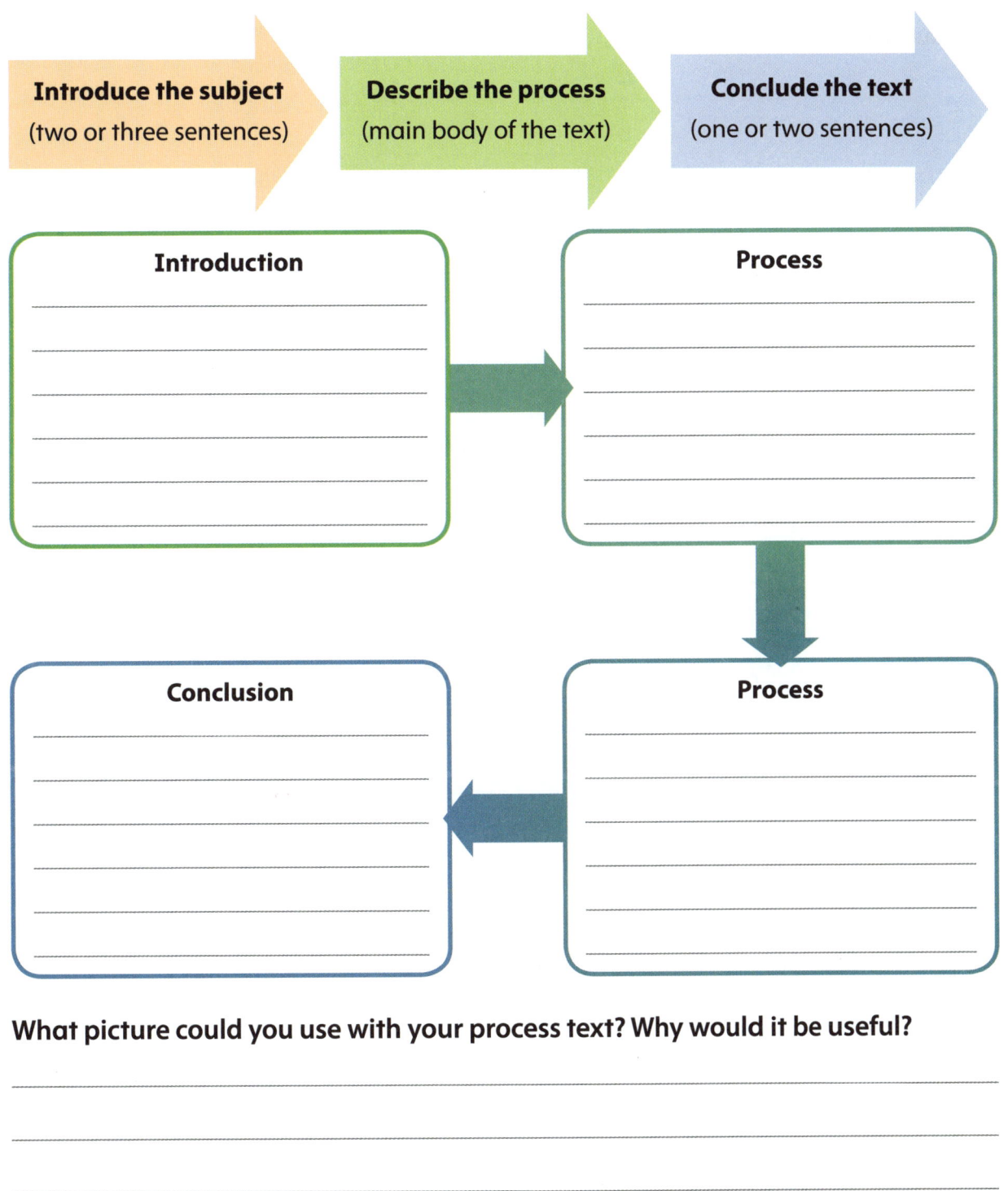

Introduce the subject
(two or three sentences)

Describe the process
(main body of the text)

Conclude the text
(one or two sentences)

Introduction

Process

Conclusion

Process

J What picture could you use with your process text? Why would it be useful?

Write Your First Draft

K Now write your process text. Use your work in activities **F** – **J** to help you.
Draw and label a diagram.

Introduction

_____

_____

_____

_____

The process

_____

_____

_____

_____

_____

_____

_____

Conclusion

_____

_____

_____

_____

Edit

L Give your process text to a partner to check.

Check your partner's spelling. Circle mistakes and write "**S**" in the margin of page 20.

Check your partner's periods and capital letters. Circle mistakes and write "**P**" in the margin of page 20.

Check your partner's vocabulary – make sure they haven't used any wrong words. Circle mistakes and write "**WW**" in the margin of page 20.

M Read and check (✓) or cross (✗).

☐ Did your partner write an introduction and a conclusion?

☐ Did your partner describe a process?

☐ Did your partner explain causes and effects, using sequence words?

Write Your Final Draft

N Correct your mistakes and write your text again on a big piece of paper. Draw and label a diagram. Display your process text in the classroom.

Write an interview with an animal

Read

A In an interview, one person asks questions for the other person to answer. Have you seen or heard an interview? Where? Now read. Do you think Ellie liked doing this interview?

An interview with a horse!

> I've always wanted to talk to my horse. I would ask him lots of questions …

Ellie   Hello, Whisper. I'm Ellie. How are you?

Whisper   I'm very happy. I've been outside in my field all day with my friends.

Ellie   That sounds nice. How do you spend the day in the field?

Whisper   We eat some grass, then we usually walk around for a while. Then we eat a bit more grass.

Ellie   Do you like being outside? It's nice and warm in your stable.

Whisper   Oh, I love being outside. We all do. It's a bit boring in the stable. I like having hay to eat, though.

Ellie   You like eating, don't you?

Whisper   Yes, I do. It's one of my favorite things.

Ellie   Do you like it when I go for a ride on you?

Whisper   Yes, it's fun, most of the time!

Ellie   What do you mean, most of the time?

Whisper   Well, sometimes you want me to trot quickly for a long time, or jump high over big poles! I like it when we plod down the road slowly!

Ellie   Sometimes you don't behave well when we go for a walk, though. Why not?

Whisper   Because I get nervous! We see cars that drive fast, and dogs that bark loudly, and they make me frightened.

Ellie   What does it mean when you put your ears back?

Whisper   Oh, do you see that? Well, that's how I express myself when I'm angry with another horse. I don't like it when another horse threatens me.

Ellie   And why do you put your ears forward?

Whisper   That means I'm listening – and that I hope you have some food for me!

Ellie   Wow! Thank you for answering my questions, Whisper!

Understand

B Circle up to five words you don't know from the text in **A**.
Check them with your teacher.

C Who is Ellie interviewing?

_____

D Write three of the questions that Ellie asks Whisper to find out what he thinks.

_____

_____

_____

E What does Ellie find out about the things Whisper likes and doesn't like?

_____

_____

_____

_____

F Look at this discussion from the interview. Circle the adverbs.

Ellie	Do you like it when I go for a ride on you?
Whisper	Yes, it's fun, most of the time!
Ellie	What do you mean, most of the time?
Whisper	Well, sometimes you want me to trot quickly for a long time, or jump high over big poles! I like it when we plod down the road slowly!

G Complete the sentences with adverbs from the text in **F**.

1 Tortoises eat plants and move very _____.

2 Cheetahs can run more _____ than any other animal.

3 Eagles are very strong and can fly _____ in the sky.

Think

H Imagine you could interview an animal. Make a list of animals that you think would be interesting.

_____

_____

I Make a list of the kind of information you would like to find out. Use the words in the box to help.

| Why   What   How   When |

_____

_____

_____

_____

J Choose the animal you want to interview. Which questions could you ask? Make notes.

_____

_____

_____

_____

_____

K Decide which answers your animal might give. Make notes. Remember, you can make the answers funny or unusual.

_____

_____

_____

_____

_____

Organize and Plan

L An interview has an opening, a middle, and an ending. Make notes, then write your questions and answers below.

Step 1: Opening
Open the interview by introducing yourself.

_____

Step 2: Questions
Ask your questions and make a note of the answers.

Question 1 _____

Answer 1 _____

Question 2 _____

Answer 2 _____

Question 3 _____

Answer 3 _____

Step 3: Ending
Close the interview by saying thank you.

_____

M **Writing Focus** Adverbs of Manner

Adverbs of manner tell us more about the way somebody does something. They can show what somebody is feeling about actions (verbs).

rudely   delicately   aggressively   bravely   calmly

How does your animal do each of their actions? Think of adverbs of manner you can use in your answers. Make notes.

_____

_____

_____

Write Your First Draft

N Now write your interview with an animal. Use your work in activities **H** – **M** to help you. Draw or glue a picture.

An Interview with _____

_____

_____

_____

_____

_____

_____

_____

_____

_____

_____

_____

_____

_____

_____

_____

_____

_____

_____

Edit

O **Give your interview to a partner to check.**

 Check your partner's simple present and present continuous verbs. Circle mistakes and write "**V**" in the margin of page 26.

 Check your partner's writing – are there any extra words? Circle mistakes and write "**X**" in the margin of page 26.

 Check your partner's vocabulary – did they choose suitable adverbs of manner to describe their verbs? Circle mistakes and write "**WW**" in the margin of page 26.

P **Read and check (✓) or cross (✗).**

☐ Did your partner introduce themselves?

☐ Did your partner write questions and answers?

☐ Did your partner use adverbs of manner in some of their answers?

☐ Did your partner thank the interviewee and close the interview?

Write Your Final Draft

Q **Correct your mistakes and write your interview again on a piece of paper. Draw or glue a picture. In pairs, read out your interview, with your partner reading the answers from the animal.**

5   Write about where things come from in the world

Read

A   An informational text gives the reader information about something. Read the text. According to the text, what are some of the advantages of getting things from other countries?

What do different countries give to the world?

Most countries share things with the rest of the world. Some countries export food, while other countries export natural resources such as oil. Some countries have invented things that people want. By sharing things, we make our lives interesting and more comfortable.

Some countries give different food to the world. Pineapples, coconuts, mangoes, and bananas come from the Caribbean and Africa, and can't be grown in Europe. Every day, we eat food from different countries.

Oil is a natural resource which is found in many countries, including Saudi Arabia, Venezuela, and North America. It is used to make gasoline, plastic, paint – even face cream and shampoo!

Televisions, computers, and mobile phones use copper, palladium, and quartz, which come from Africa and South America. There are different natural resources in different countries.

Many countries share their inventions and cultural activities with the world. For example, Norway was the first country to introduce skiing to foreign tourists. Spain gave the world the guitar, and Italy gave the world the violin and the opera. These inventions and cultural activities tell us something about the countries they came from.

In conclusion, different countries give the world things such as food, resources, activities, and inventions, which teach us about their culture and make our world more interesting.

Understand

B Circle up to five words you don't know from the text in **A**.
Check them with your teacher.

C Look at the informational text. What is the purpose of the first paragraph?

_____

D Which of the topics below are discussed in the text in **A**? Check (✓) or cross (✗).
Then number the checked topics in the order they appear in the text.

☐☐ language	☐☐ people	☐☐ jobs
☐☐ animals	✓① food	☐☐ sport
☐☐ music	☐☐ health	☐☐ natural resources

E Read these sentences from paragraph 4 of the text in **A**. Number them in order.

☐ Spain gave the world the guitar, and Italy gave the world the violin and the opera.

☐ For example, Norway was the first country to introduce skiing to foreign tourists.

☐ Many countries share their inventions and cultural activities with the world.

☐ These inventions and cultural activities tell us something about the countries they came from.

F Look at the text in **A** again and think about the order in which the information is given. Then read these sentences and number them in the correct order.

☐ They were the first people to invent paper money, fireworks, and ammunition.

☐ So, while in the past, their inventions and artwork have made the Chinese famous, today it has been their cuisine.

☐ Their craftsmen sold silks and beautiful pottery to Europe.

☐ In the past 2000 years, the Chinese have given the world a wide range of things.

☐ However, in modern times, it is Chinese food that has become a famous cultural export.

Think

G Think of three different examples for each of the topics in the table. Write.

music and dance	jazz, salsa, reggae
foods	
clothing	
sports	
inventions	
natural resources	

H Think about your answers in **G**. Do you know or can you find out which country created each example? Write.

_____

_____

_____

_____

_____

I Choose three topics from **G** that you'd like to write about.
Complete the chart with the examples and where they come from.
Do any of them come from the same country?

	Topic 1: _____	Topic 2: _____	Topic 3: _____
Example 1	_____ from _____	_____ from _____	_____ from _____
Example 2	_____ from _____	_____ from _____	_____ from _____
Example 3	_____ from _____	_____ from _____	_____ from _____

Organize and Plan

J The informational text in **A** can be divided into five paragraphs:

Paragraph 1	Introduction
Paragraph 2	Food
Paragraph 3	Natural resources
Paragraph 4	Cultural activities
Paragraph 5	Conclusion

K Look at your chart in **I**. Use your ideas to choose the topics for paragraphs 2–4 of your informational text.

Paragraph 2 topic:

_____

Paragraph 3 topic:

_____

Paragraph 4 topic:

_____

L 🔍 **Writing Focus** Topic, Supporting, and Concluding Sentences

In an informational text, information must be presented clearly. Each paragraph should follow this structure:

topic sentence → **two or three supporting sentences** → **concluding sentence**

The **supporting sentences** give more information about the **topic sentence**. The **concluding sentence** summarizes the information in the paragraph.

Make notes about the content of paragraphs 2–4 of your text. Think about a topic sentence, supporting sentences, and a concluding sentence.

Paragraph 2

_____

_____

Paragraph 3

_____

_____

Paragraph 4

_____

_____

Write Your First Draft

M Now write your informational text. Use your work in activities **G** – **L** to help you. Find and glue a picture.

Edit

N Give your informational text to a partner to check.

Check your partner's periods and capital letters. Circle mistakes and write "**P**" in the margin of page 32.

Check your partner's writing – is it separated into paragraphs? Circle where a new paragraph should start and write "**[**" in the margin of page 32.

Check your partner's writing – are there any missing words? Circle mistakes and write "**M**" in the margin of page 32.

O Read and check (✓) or cross (✗).

☐ Did your partner write an introduction?

☐ Did your partner order their paragraphs into a topic sentence, supporting sentences, and a concluding sentence?

☐ Did your partner write a conclusion?

Write Your Final Draft

P Correct your mistakes and type your text on a computer. Add a picture. In small groups, read out your texts. Think. What interesting things did you learn? Tell a person from another group.

Write a descriptive text

Read

A Personification gives human qualities to objects, animals, or other nonliving things. Can you think of a story that uses personification? Now read this descriptive text. Have you ever been to a place like this?

It's springtime, and walkers are gradually starting to visit the mountains again after the long winter season. Walking down the mountain, the stream rushes past us, leaping and jumping over jagged rocks and stones. High above, skylarks are hovering and singing. Their bubbling song echoes the stream's gentle laughter.

On warm spring days like this, people love to walk here and eat picnics on the mountainside. No one is brave enough yet to test the icy waters and go for a swim. Seeing the trees' long fingers reach down and skim the surface of the water, it is tempting to stop and rest here, but we're heading down the mountain and we can't stop yet. From here, it's only another half an hour until we reach our destination in the sleeping valley below. We have a favorite spot by the river bank where we can lie in the sun and listen to the first whispers of spring.

Understand

B Circle up to five words you don't know from the text in **A**.
Check them with your teacher.

C What is the author describing in this text?

_____

_____

D Read these sentences from the text in **A**. The words in bold are examples
of personification. Reread the text and find another sentence containing
personification. Then write that sentence below.

1 Walking down the mountain, the stream rushes past us, **leaping** and **jumping** …

2 High above, skylarks are hovering and singing. Their bubbling song echoes
the stream's gentle **laughter**.

3 Seeing the trees' long **fingers** reach down and skim the surface of the water,
it is tempting to stop and rest here …

4 We have a favorite spot by the river bank where we can lie in the sun and
listen to the first **whispers** of spring.

_____

_____

E We can personify a text with nouns, verbs, or adjectives. Read the first
paragraph below. Then read texts A and B. How do these two different
examples of personification make you feel in comparison to the original?

_____

It's a quiet evening. There's a dark storm on the horizon. The gray
clouds are gathering and soon the rain will pour on the silent town.

A It's a **restless** evening. There's **an angry**
storm on the horizon. The **scowling**
clouds are **arguing** and soon the rain
will **scream at** the **crazy** town.

B It's a **thoughtful** evening. There's
a sleepy storm on the horizon. The
calm clouds are **whispering** and soon
the rain will **wake** the **sleeping** town.

Think

F Think of experiences in your life. Use the ideas below to help you make notes.

What?	a walk? a sailing trip? a picnic? _____ _____
Where?	the mountains? a beach? a forest? _____ _____
Features	sky? clouds? trees? lake? buildings? _____ _____

G Choose an activity, a place, and the features you want to describe from **F**. Write.

_____

_____

_____

H **Writing Focus** **Personification**

Personification means to use words that could describe a person. You can use adjectives, verbs, and nouns to personify a text.

The **smiling** mountain **stretched** high into the sky, and we felt its **joy** as it **touched** the clouds.

Make notes about how you could personify one of the features you will describe. Use your notebook to make notes about more features.

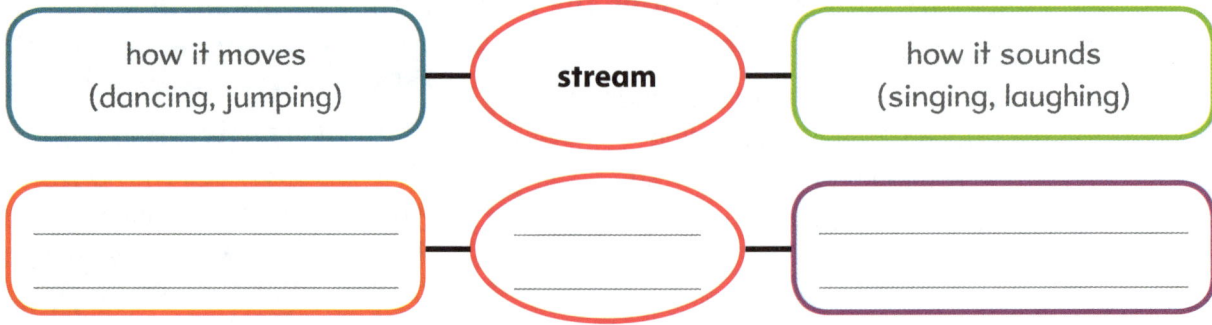

how it moves (dancing, jumping) — stream — how it sounds (singing, laughing)

Organize and Plan

I Think of how you want to plan your text. Remember to describe a variety of of features in the order they are seen.

> **Where?**
> _____
> _____
> _____

> **When? (What season is it? What time of day is it?)**
> _____
> _____
> _____

> **Who?**
> _____
> _____
> _____

> **What are you doing / seeing?**
> _____
> _____
> _____

J Read **E** again. Think of how you want to personify your description. Choose some ideas from your notes in **H**.

_____
_____
_____
_____
_____

Write Your First Draft

K Now write your descriptive text. Use your work in activities **F** – **J** to help you. Draw or glue a picture.

Edit

L Give your descriptive text to a partner to check.

S Check your partner's spelling. Circle mistakes and write "**S**" in the margin of page 38.

V Check your partner's simple present and present continuous verbs. Circle mistakes and write "**V**" in the margin of page 38.

WO Check your partner's word order – make sure that nouns come after adjectives. Circle mistakes and write "**WO**" in the margin of page 38.

M Read and check (✓) or cross (✗).

☐ Did your partner write about a setting?

☐ Did your partner describe more than one feature of the setting?

☐ Did your partner use adjectives, verbs, and nouns to personify their text?

Write Your Final Draft

N Correct your mistakes and write your text again in your notebook. Draw or glue a picture. Read out your text to the class.

Write about a hypothetical situation

7

Read

A A hypothetical text asks the readers to put themselves in an imaginary situation. Can you think of a hypothetical text? Now read. Do you think the situation in the text will ever happen?

A

Have you ever wondered what it would be like to live in a world without money? If you didn't have money, you wouldn't be able to buy anything. How would you eat or keep warm? Where would you live? How would you survive?

B

In the past, people bartered and traded goods they had for things they wanted. If you grew more food than you needed, you could trade it for something that you wanted. For example, you could trade apples for some cheese, or ten potatoes for a basket. If you didn't have anything to trade, you could trade your labor. For instance, you could work for a farmer in exchange for food or shelter. But, if we went back to that system, who would decide the "value" of anything? Who would decide that building houses is more valuable than making clothes, or that ten potatoes has the value of one basket?

C

It would probably be very difficult to live without money, because eventually labor, skills, and goods would start to have a value. A person with a horse, which could be used for transport, would have more trading value than a person with a cat. A person with twenty apples would be richer than a person with five apples. In the end, perhaps it would be impossible to live without money, and society would have to invent a different form of exchange that was similar to money.

Understand

B Circle up to five words you don't know from the text in **A**. Check them with your teacher.

C What imaginary situation does the text talk about?

_____

D The hypothetical text in **A** has three paragraphs. Match the titles below to paragraphs A, B, and C, and complete them in the text.

- ⬜ Trade your goods and skills
- ⬜ A different way of paying for things
- ⬜ What would it be like to live without money?

E We use conditional tenses to talk about hypothetical situations. Circle the conditional tenses in these sentences from the text.

1 If you (didn't have) money, you (wouldn't be) able to buy anything.

2 If you grew more food than you needed, you could trade it for something that you wanted.

3 If you didn't have anything to trade, you could trade your labor.

4 It would probably be very difficult to live without money, because eventually labor, skills, and goods would start to have a value.

F Read this paragraph about a world without money. Change the verbs in brackets to the conditional tense, using *would*.

In a world without money, people
_____would help_____ (help) their neighbors
and friends more. People _____ (work) for
free for their local community. It _____ (is)
impossible for anyone to have more power than anyone else
just because they had more money. If you wanted anything,
you _____ (trade) your skills.

Think

G **Writing Focus** Conditional Tenses

When we discuss hypothetical questions, we need to use **conditional tenses**. These can describe imaginary situations.

What would it be like if ... ?

If we didn't have ... , we would have to ...

People wouldn't be able to ... if they didn't ...

The text in **A** asks hypothetical questions about money. What other topics could you ask hypothetical questions about? Write.

_____

_____

_____

H What hypothetical questions can you ask about your topics from **G**?

1 _____

2 _____

3 _____

I Can you think of answers to your hypothetical questions from **H**?

_____

_____

_____

J Choose your best hypothetical question from **H**. What could the outcome be? Write.

Organize and Plan

k There are three paragraphs in the hypothetical text in **A**. Read this paragraph plan and make notes about how you will group your ideas.

Paragraph 1:
Main question and secondary questions

Paragraph 2:
Discuss what people could or would do

Paragraph 3:
Concluding statement

Paragraph 1: Main question and secondary questions

What would it be like if … ?

How would … ?   What would … ?   Where would … ?

_____

_____

_____

_____

Paragraph 2: Discuss what people could or would do

People could …   If we didn't … , we couldn't …

Nobody would …   There wouldn't be …

_____

_____

_____

_____

Paragraph 3: Concluding statement

I think …   It would (probably) be …

_____

_____

_____

_____

Write Your First Draft

L Now write your hypothetical text. Use your work in activities **G** – **K** to help you. Draw or glue a picture.

Paragraph 1 _____
_____
_____
_____
_____
_____
_____

Paragraph 2 _____
_____
_____
_____
_____

Paragraph 3 _____
_____
_____
_____
_____
_____
_____

Edit

M Give your hypothetical text to a partner to check.

 Check your partner's conditional verbs. Circle mistakes and write "**V**" in the margin of page 44.

 Check your partner's writing – are there any missing words? Circle mistakes and write "**M**" in the margin of page 44.

 Check your partner's vocabulary – make sure they haven't used any wrong words. Circle mistakes and write "**WW**" in the margin of page 44.

N Read and check (✓) or cross (✗).

☐ Did your partner ask and answer hypothetical questions?

☐ Did your partner write main questions and secondary questions?

☐ Did your partner write their opinions in a concluding statement?

Write Your Final Draft

O Correct your mistakes and write your text again on a piece of paper. Draw or glue a picture. Put all the hypothetical texts from the class together into a book. As a class, think of a title for the book.

Read

A An engaging story is a story that captures your attention by being interesting and exciting. Can you think of a story like this? Now read. What do you think is behind the door?

The Door in the Woods

My dog Alfie had been running through the woods ahead of me, but suddenly he stopped. He made a strange noise, and wouldn't move. I looked, and saw a mysterious thing. There, between two trees, was a door. I couldn't remember seeing it before, but it looked very old – ancient – with paint peeling off, and a massive, rusty iron handle. The door was slightly open, but I couldn't see what was on the other side.

As I looked, Alfie began to bark, and his ears twitched. A small rabbit was sitting next to one of the trees. It froze for a moment, staring at Alfie.

Alfie paused, then darted forward as the rabbit ran away, disappearing through the door. Alfie slipped through the door, out of my sight. I called him back, but he didn't hear me – or if he did, he didn't come back.

For a second, I could still hear him barking. Then everything went quiet. Even the birds overhead fell silent. I looked at the door nervously, but I knew I had to go through to find him, perhaps to save him. Slowly, I took a step towards it …

Understand

B Circle up to five words you don't know from the text in **A**.
Check them with your teacher.

C An engaging story should have these five elements. Read these
definitions and choose the correct word.

1   a beginning that grabs the reader's attention   **conflict / hook**

2   the people or animals in a story   **characters / plot**

3   the main events in a story   **hook / plot**

4   a problem in a story that needs to be solved or fixed   **characters / conflict**

5   a surprising or shocking end to a paragraph, chapter, or story   **conflict / cliffhanger**

D Read the story in **A** again. Match the elements from **C** to these
descriptions of the story.

a   The boy's dog is missing after going through the door.   _____

b   A boy sees a strange door in the woods.   _____

c   There's a boy and his dog, Alfie.   _____

d   A boy is walking through the woods and he sees a door.
The dog starts barking and it runs through the door.
The boy steps closer to the door and wonders what to
do next.   _____

e   Suddenly the dog's barking gets quiet. Even the birds
are silent. Then the boy takes a step closer.   _____

E An engaging story needs to be interesting. Look at sentences A and B.
How are they different?

> **A** An engaging story should leap into your reader's mind, powerfully
> grab their attention, and rapidly tell them something interesting.
>
> **B** An engaging story should get your reader's attention.

_____

_____

Circle the words that make sentence A a more engaging sentence.

Think

F Think of two ideas for your own engaging story. Write.

_____

_____

G Think about the elements you learned in **C**. Can you make notes on these elements for each of your story ideas from **F**?

Hook
- _____
- _____

Plot
- _____

  _____
- _____

  _____

Characters
- _____
- _____

Cliffhanger
- _____

  _____
- _____

  _____

Conflict
- _____
- _____

H 🔍 **Writing Focus**   Enriching Language

In an engaging story, the writer chooses verbs, adverbs, and adjectives that make the writing more engaging and enriching.

He scrambled frantically over the wall, and leaped into the little boat with only seconds to spare before the gang could reach him.

Think of how you can use language to make your ideas more interesting. Make notes.

_____

_____

_____

_____

Organize and Plan

I Choose your best idea from **F** and make more detailed notes.

Hook	
Characters	
Conflict	
Plot	
Cliffhanger	

J Think about how many paragraphs you want to write and order your ideas within each paragraph.

Paragraph 1

_____

_____

_____

Paragraph 2

_____

_____

_____

Paragraph 3

_____

_____

_____

Write Your First Draft

K Now write your engaging story. Use your work in activities **F** – **J** to help you. Draw or glue a picture.

Edit

L Give your engaging story to a partner to check.

 Check your partner's periods and capital letters. Circle mistakes and write "**P**" in the margin of page 50.

 Check your partner's writing – is it separated into paragraphs? Circle where a new paragraph should start and write "**[**" in the margin of page 50.

 Check your partner's word order – make sure that nouns come after adjectives. Circle mistakes and write "**WO**" in the margin of page 50.

M Read and check (✓) or cross (✗).

- ☐ Does your partner's story start with a hook to get the reader's attention?
- ☐ Did your partner include a conflict to add interest?
- ☐ Does your partner's story end with a cliffhanger?
- ☐ Did your partner use exciting language to engage the reader?

Write Your Final Draft

N Correct your mistakes and write your story again in your notebook. Draw or glue a picture. Read out your story to the class. As a class, talk about cliffhanger endings. Do you think this is a good way to end a story?

Write about how a building is made

Read

A A process report explains to the reader how something is done. Can you think of any process reports? Now read. Would you like to live in this type of house? Why or why not?

Straw Bale House

This type of house is environmentally friendly because it's warm in the winter, cool in the summer, cheap to heat, and very cheap to build. The most unusual thing about it is that it's made of straw!

First, the foundations are built. Then, the outer timber frame of the house is constructed. The frame is nailed together.

The roof frame can be built at the same time and can be put aside until the walls are built. Next, the four walls are built using straw bales. A complete layer of bales is set around the edge of the base, inside the frame. The walls are built upward, with the bales stacked in overlapping rows like bricks. They are held together using long wooden stakes. As the walls are constructed, the windows, plumbing, and electrics are fitted in the usual way. This is also the time when the wooden floor and stairs are fitted.

Last, the roof frame is lifted into position and attached to the straw walls, using wooden stakes. The roof frame is covered with tiles or thatch. When it is finished, the inside and outside walls are rendered with plaster.

Understand

B Circle up to five words you don't know from the text in **A**.
Check them with your teacher.

C Which of these materials are used when making a straw bale house? Circle.

> iron   straw bales   bricks   plaster   concrete   wood   plastic

D What is the first thing that is completed when building a straw bale house?

_____

E Check the correct sequence of adverbs.

☐ First, Next, Last, Then   ☐ First, Then, Next, Last

F Look at sentences 1 and 2. How are they different? Complete the sentence below using *active* and *passive*.

1 We made the house with straw.   **2** The house is made with straw.

Sentence 1 uses the _____ voice, and sentence 2 uses the _____ voice.

G Read these instructions for building a brick wall. Then rewrite the paragraph as a report using the passive voice.

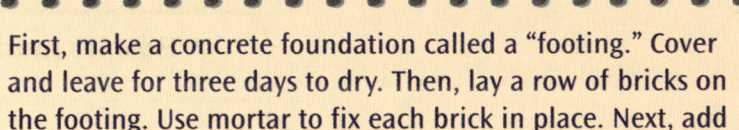

First, make a concrete foundation called a "footing." Cover and leave for three days to dry. Then, lay a row of bricks on the footing. Use mortar to fix each brick in place. Next, add more layers of bricks until the wall is finished. Last, remove any excess mortar with a brush.

First, a concrete foundation called a "footing" is made.

_____

_____

_____

_____

_____

Think

H Look at the types of building. Make notes about the materials you need to make each one, and what is unusual about them.

Skyscraper	Grass hut

Igloo	Ice hotel

I Choose one of the buildings from **H**. Do you know or can you find out:

1 ⬜ how it is made?

2 ⬜ the correct order of stages to make this building?

J Write your building choice in the center of the diagram below. Complete the diagram with your ideas.

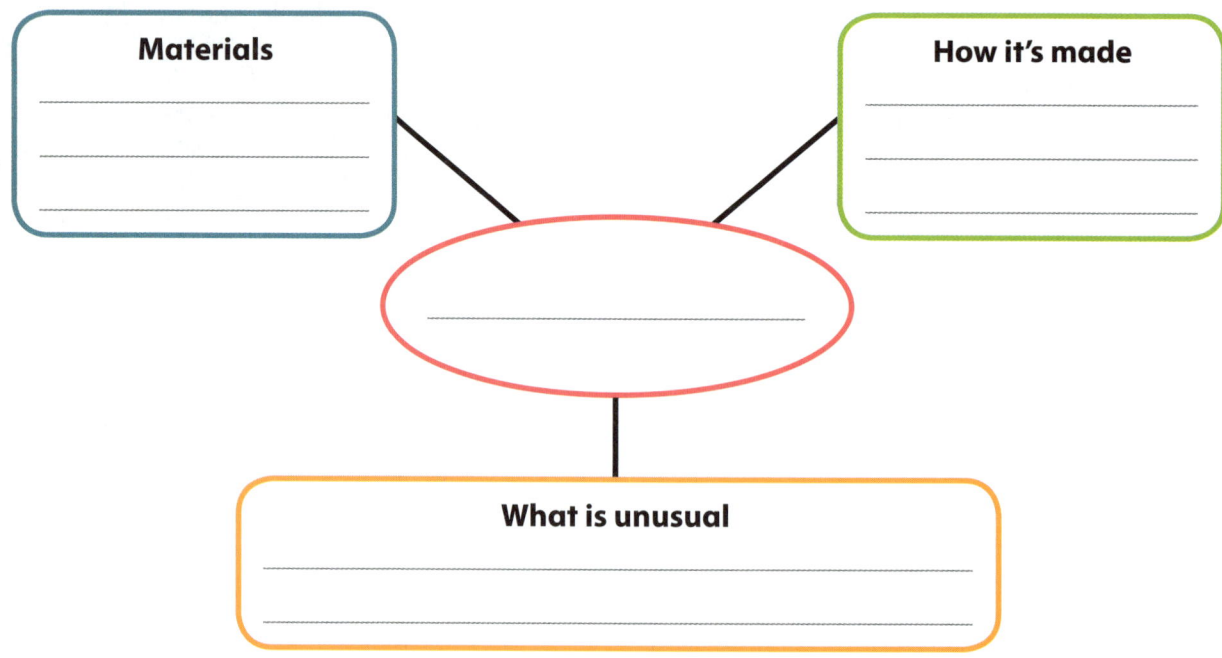

Materials

How it's made

What is unusual

Organize and Plan

K When you have a sequence of events, it helps to group them into stages. Look at this example from **A**.

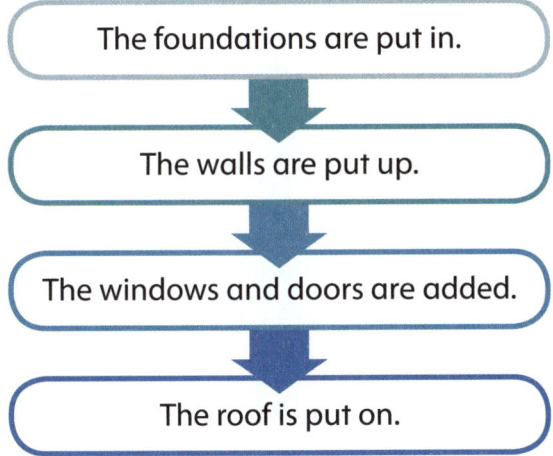

The foundations are put in.

The walls are put up.

The windows and doors are added.

The roof is put on.

Make notes about how your building is made. Put the stages in the correct order. Use the adverbs of sequence in the box to help.

Then	Last	First	Next

_____

_____

_____

_____

L 🔍 **Writing Focus**   **Passive Voice to Describe a Process**

In a process report, the **passive voice** is used to describe the different stages.

First, the foundations are laid. Then, the bricks are placed in a row.

What verbs will you need to use in the passive to describe your process? Make notes.

_____

_____

_____

_____

Write Your First Draft

M Now write your process report. Use your work in activities **H** – **L** to help you. Find and glue a picture.

Edit

N Give your process report to a partner to check.

Check your partner's spelling. Circle mistakes and write "**S**" in the margin of page 56.

Check your partner's verbs in the passive voice. Circle mistakes and write "**V**" in the margin of page 56.

Check your partner's writing – are there any extra words? Circle mistakes and write "**X**" in the margin of page 56.

O Read and check (✓) or cross (✗).

☐ Did your partner describe a sequence of events?

☐ Did your partner order these events correctly?

☐ Did your partner use adverbs of sequence to order the stages of their process?

☐ Did your partner use the passive voice to describe each different stage?

Write Your Final Draft

P Correct your mistakes and type your report on a computer. Add a picture. In small groups, say what type of building your report is about. Then describe your process in three or four sentences, with one sentence for each stage of the process.

Error Correction Master Class

A Read the text. What type of text is it? What is it about?

B Look at the error codes in the box below. Then look at each mistake in the text and the error code in the margin. Work with a partner to decide the correct answers.

S – Spelling mistake	P – Punctuation mistake
V – Verb mistake	M – Missing word
X – Extra word	WW – Wrong word
WO – Wrong word order	[– New paragraph should start

How do animals hear?

M — Most living things can hear, but they do it in lots different and interesting ways. Sounds travel through the air, water, and ground, and those sound signals need to reach the brain so that animals

[— can hear the world outside. Many animals can hear sounds that humans can't. Bats need to move in the dark so they can hear

V — sounds that bounced off walls, and this helps them know where the surface is. This is really important for bats because they are nearly blind!

S — Not all animals have ears. Snakes feel sounds through there skin. Most insects pick up sounds through tiny hairs on their body. Fish feel sounds as the waves move through the water.

X — Elephants do have ears, and a very good hearing. But they also

WW — use their ears in other reasons. Their ears are very large and this

P — helps to regulate their body temperature, keeping them cool

So, many animals have ears that are different from ours or

WO — can hear with parts different of their body. They also hear a wide variety of sounds. The animal world is very interesting!

C Write the text correctly in your notebook.

D Look at the error codes in **B**. Read the text below. Work with a partner to find and circle 15 mistakes. Write the correct error code in the margin.

What would we do without education?

Have ever you thought about a world where you didn't have to go to school? If you didn't go to school, you woldn't have lots of different friends. How you would learn different subjects, and what would you do all the day? A long time ago, children didn't go to school. They would go out to work with their parents, helping to bring crops from the feilds or doing chores around the house. It didn't mean they had a lot of free time because they are still very busy. How did they learn about the wider world and learn new skills to help them find a job.

These days, I think it would be difficult learn enough skills if you didn't go to school. You couldn't learn to be doctor or about sience. Also, children allowed aren't to work now, so what would you did all day? And, if your parents worked, who would look for you?

in the end, I think that school is necessary because you find out important things about the world, and it helps prepare you for the future.

E Now write the text correctly in your notebook.

Spelling Master Class

1 Suffixes -ible, -able, -ibly, -ably

A ○ Spelling Focus

We can add the suffixes **-ible**, **-able**, **-ibly**, **-ably** to verbs and nouns, to make adjectives or adverbs.

-ible and **-able** are the adjective forms.   **-ibly** and **-ably** are the adverb forms.

Match the adjectives to the adverbs.

1 predictable ●   ● **a** flexibly

2 flexible ●   ● **b** terribly

3 valuable ●   ● **c** valuably

4 terrible ●   ● **d** predictably

B Use the words in the box to complete the sentence.

> *y*   adverb   *e*   adjective

When the _____ ends with *-able* and *-ible,* we delete _____ and we add _____ to make the _____ .

C Complete the adjectives with *-ible* or *-able*. Use a dictionary if you need help.

1 vulner __ __ __ __   3 ed __ __ __ __   5 revers __ __ __ __

2 prefer __ __ __ __   4 desir __ __ __ __   6 leg __ __ __ __

D Write the adverbs for these adjectives. Then complete the sentences.

1 amicable   _____   3 responsible   _____

2 incredible   _____   4 comfortable   _____

a The students felt scared but behaved _____ , and called the police.

b The two teams shook hands _____ after the game.

c Lucy settled herself _____ into her armchair and began reading.

d The firefighters who entered the burning building were _____ brave.

2 Prefix un-

🔍 Spelling Focus

To make a word with the opposite meaning or
a negative meaning, we can add the prefix **un-**:

tie   **un**tie
happy   **un**happy

B Write the adjectives again using *un-*. Then complete the sentences.

1 well _____   **4** wrapped _____

2 comfortable _____   **5** certain _____

3 safe _____   **6** pleasant _____

a Matthew was _____ about what he should do next.

b Isabel felt _____, so she stayed in bed that day.

c Carrie's shoes were too small and very _____.

d The smell from the garbage was _____.

e Our presents for Mom were _____, but she didn't mind.

f Cycling without a helmet is _____.

C Complete the text using four of the words below. You will need to add *un-* to some of the words.

expected   pack   friendly   cover   lucky   finished

Ben was on a trip to Italy. He was staying with the Rossi family, who all seemed really
nice and _____. There were two boys in the family – Marco and Gianni.
On Ben's first day, Marco helped him to _____ his suitcase and showed
him everything in the house. Then Marco's mom took them downtown. Ben was
excited and felt very _____ to be in such a beautiful place. When they
got to the main square, Ben suddenly saw one of his friends from school. It was so
_____! They said hi and agreed to meet the next day.

3 Prefixes *pre-* and *pro-*

A ○ Spelling Focus

Many words start with **pre-** and **pro-**. You have to learn the different spellings.

Use the letters *e* or *o* to complete each word below. Use a dictionary if you need help.

1 pr ___ cess

2 pr ___ servation

3 pr ___ digy

4 pr ___ claim

5 pr ___ pelling

6 pr ___ perty

7 pr ___ view

8 pr ___ motion

9 pr ___ dictable

B Complete the words in the sentences with *pre-* or *pro-*.

1 Before he left, Cameron ___ ___ ___ mised to be careful.

2 It was late, and Max ___ ___ ___ tended to be asleep.

3 Three players stood in Ben's way and ___ ___ ___ vented him from scoring.

4 A mother bear always tries to ___ ___ ___ tect her cubs.

5 Mary liked cookies, but her brother ___ ___ ___ ferred candy.

6 Brad wanted to become a ___ ___ ___ fessional tennis player.

C Complete the words with *pre-* or *pro-* . Then complete the text with five of these words.

1 ___ ___ ___ gress

2 ___ ___ ___ blems

3 ___ ___ ___ historic

4 ___ ___ ___ ject

5 ___ ___ ___ parations

6 ___ ___ ___ nounce

7 ___ ___ ___ vious

8 ___ ___ ___ duce

9 ___ ___ ___ fessor

The teacher told her class that they would be doing a new _____ on dinosaurs and other _____ animals. She wanted each of them to _____ a really good piece of work, which they could display in the school hall. First, all the students had to think about their ideas carefully and get their materials ready. The teacher helped them with these _____ . Then the students began their work. They all made good _____ and finished on time.

4 Spelling with *ie* and *ei*

A   Spelling Focus

You often find the letters **ie** and **ei** in the middle of a word.
There are some rules to help you remember the correct order.

Look at the chart. Circle *ie* and *ei* in the words.

Words	Rules
field, thief, niece, piece, friend, interview, _____	_____ _____
receive, ceiling, perceive, _____	_____ _____
ancient, eight, freight, neighbor, _____	_____ _____

B   Look at the rules. Write them in the chart in A.

write *ei* after *c*   some words don't follow a rule   in general, write *ie*

C   Write the words below in the correct place in the chart in A.

species   deceive   pierce

D   Use the letters *ie* or *ei* to complete the words. Then complete the sentences with four of these words.

1 s __ __ ze   **3** sc __ __ nce   **5** n__ __ ther

2 w __ __ rd   **4** conc __ __ ted   **6** suffic __ __ nt

a I didn't have any money, and _____ did Jennifer.

b Tom found his _____ classes very interesting.

c There was a _____ sound coming from the yard.

d The singer was very arrogant and _____ .

5 Homophones

A Spelling Focus

Homophones are words that sound the same, but which are spelled differently.

by   **buy**   **one**   **won**

Write the words next to their homophones.

who's   four   there   you're   two   it's

1 too _____

2 their _____

3 its _____

4 whose _____

5 your _____

6 for _____

B Write a homophone for each word. Then complete the sentences with the homophones.

1 blue _____

2 sail _____

3 meat _____

4 pear _____

5 groan _____

6 sun _____

a Laura went to _____ her friend at the shopping mall.

b The wind _____ so hard that the trees bent over.

c Mr. and Mrs. Ashman had two daughters and one _____.

d The poor man only had one _____ of shoes.

e "You've _____ so tall!" said Lucy's grandmother.

f Many houses were for _____ in the same street.

C Look at the words in the box. Think of their homophones. Then complete the text with the four correct words.

eight   past   whether   hole   sea   right

The Collins family had a wonderful vacation. All week, the _____ was hot, and they didn't _____ a single cloud in the sky. Everyone just wanted to relax, and so they often spent the _____ day either swimming or lying next to the pool. Every evening, they _____ dinner at a different restaurant. It was great!

6 Mnemonics

A 🔍 **Spelling Strategy**

A **mnemonic** device is a sentence or rhyme that helps you to remember a spelling rule. Here are some examples:

u always follows **q**.
Hear or here? You **hear** with your **ear**.

B What spelling strategy does this mnemonic device help you with?

When it says "ee",
put *i* before *e*
but not after *c*.

_____

C This mnemonic helps you to remember how to spell a word. Write the word.

Big **E**lephants **C**an **A**lways **U**nderstand **S**mall **E**lephants.

_____

D Match the words and their mnemonics.

1 would ●   ● **a** I **ate** my dinner immedi**ate**ly.

2 immediately ●   ● **b** Silly **ant** is **d**ancing.

3 believe ●   ● **c** You need a *u* in "would you like."

4 said ●   ● **d** Don't bel**ie**ve a **lie**.

E Think of a word that you find hard to spell. Write it.

_____

F Write a mnemonic for the word in **E**.

_____

_____

A **Spelling Focus**

We can change the meaning of a word by putting **in-** or **im-** at the beginning.

Match the word pairs and circle *in-* or *im-*.

1 polite ●		● **a**	inaccurate
2 correct ●		● **b**	impossible
3 accurate ●		● **c**	incapable
4 mature ●		● **e**	imperfect
5 possible ●		● **f**	invisible
6 perfect ●		● **g**	incorrect
7 capable ●		● **h**	impolite
8 visible ●		● **i**	immature

B How do the prefixes *in-* and *im-* usually change the meaning of a word? Check (✓).

☐ They change the word to mean "bad."

☐ They change the word to mean "not … ."

C Add the prefix *in-* or *im-* to these adjectives. Then complete the sentences with the words. Use a dictionary if you need help.

1 __ __ measurable **3** __ __ complete **5** __ __ mobile

2 __ __ convenient **4** __ __ ventive **6** __ __ patient

a It was _____ for the whole family when the car needed repairs.

b The man was _____ and wanted to leave immediately.

c The number of grains of sand on a beach is _____ .

d She was an _____ designer, who always had fun ideas.

e After her operation, Anna was _____ for two weeks.

f The puzzle was _____ , and Sam could not find the missing piece.

8 Suffixes –ous and –ious

A ○ Spelling Focus

We can add **-ous** or **-ious** to the end of some nouns to make adjectives:

danger   dang**erous**
grace   grac**ious**

Complete the adjectives with *-ous* or *-ious*. Use a dictionary if you need help.

1 space   spac ___ ___ ___ ___
2 moment   moment ___ ___ ___
3 nerve   nerv ___ ___ ___
4 carnivore carnivor ___ ___ ___
5 fury   fur ___ ___ ___ ___

6 poison   poison ___ ___ ___
7 envy   env ___ ___ ___ ___
8 adventure adventur ___ ___ ___
9 mystery   myster ___ ___ ___ ___
10 humor   humor ___ ___ ___

B Look at the words in Ⓐ. Write the adjectives in the chart.

+ *ous*	
delete e + ious	
delete y + ious	
delete e + ous	

C Write the adjectives for these nouns, using *-ous* or *-ious*. Then complete the sentences with the words.

1 melody   _____
2 mountain   _____
3 study   _____

4 fame   _____
5 victory   _____
6 ridicule   _____

a After three months of fighting, the army was finally _____.

b The route was very _____ and only the best hikers were chosen.

c James looked _____ when he dressed up as a pineapple.

d Laura was extremely _____ and always did well at school.

e Many people who are on television regularly are _____.

f The tune that the orchestra was playing was very _____.

9 Keep a Spelling Log

A 🔍 Spelling Strategy

A spelling log is a list of difficult words. When we want
to remember a difficult word, we can write a note or
a mnemonic device, or we can draw a picture to help:

ate	eat, ate, eaten
poor	oo = not rich
receive	put i before e but not after c

B Match the words to these spelling notes.

1 queen ●   ● a   I s👁👁 you.

2 four ●   ● b   e + ous

3 courageous ●   ● c   4

4 see ●   ● d   u follows q.

C Think of some difficult words. Look at the spelling notes in **A**. How can you remember your difficult words? Write your ideas.

_____

_____

_____

_____

D Write your spelling log. Use your ideas from **C**. You can draw pictures in your notebook.

Difficult word	Spelling notes

Wordlist

This wordlist contains useful words from this book. Use the space to add translations or explanations to help you remember them.

Module 1

breeding _____

destruction _____

fragile _____

funds _____

precious _____

rare _____

slaughter _____

survival _____

vital _____

vulnerable _____

Module 2

beak _____

beaver _____

blowhole _____

nostrils _____

otter _____

signal _____

snout _____

tool _____

trunk _____

Module 3

axle _____

belts _____

blade _____

dammed _____

force _____

gears _____

industry _____

mill _____

rotate _____

sluice _____

transmit _____

turbine _____

Module 4

express _____

hay _____

plod _____

pole _____

stable _____

threaten _____

Module 5

copper _____

cultural _____

export _____

foreign _____

palladium _____

resource _____

quartz _____

Module 6

echo _____

hover _____

jagged _____

laughter _____

leaping _____

skim _____

skylark _____

tempting _____

valley _____

Module 7

barter _____

basket _____

exchange _____

goods _____

labor _____

skill _____

society _____

trade _____

value _____

Module 8

ancient _____

froze _____

handle _____

massive _____

pause _____

peeling _____

rusty _____

twitch _____

save _____

Module 9

bale _____

constructed _____

foundations _____

layer _____

overlapping _____

plaster _____

rendered _____

straw _____

thatch _____

timber _____

Great Clarendon Street, Oxford, OX2 6DP, United Kingdom

Oxford University Press is a department of the University of Oxford.
It furthers the University's objective of excellence in research, scholarship,
and education by publishing worldwide. Oxford is a registered trade
mark of Oxford University Press in the UK and in certain other countries

ISBN: 978 0 19 405287 0

Printed in China

This book is printed on paper from certified and well-managed sources

ACKNOWLEDGEMENTS

Back cover photograph: Oxford University Press building/David Fisher

Front cover photograph: chuyu/123RF (Shanghai)

Illustrations by: Dave Hill pp.15, 16, 22, 45, 46, 51.

The publisher would like to thank the following for permission to reproduce photographs:
Alamy pp.4 (George H.H. Huey), (turtle/George H.H. Huey), 5 (David Da Costa),
9 (collecting water/Melvyn Longhurst), (penguins covered in oil/John Moulds),
11 (David Chapman), 29 (Simon Curtis), 39 (sailing boat/Lphoto), 52 (Adrian
Sherratt); Getty Images pp.27 (tiger/Steven Poe), 33 (origami/nikoniko_happy),
(sushi/William Reavell), 53 (Simon Battensby); Oxford University Press
pp.10 (Corel), 21 (riding bike/Shutterstock; greenland), 27 (camel/123rf/David
Steele), 35 (Photodisc), 40 (Photodisc); Rex Features p.41 (c.Paramount/Everett);
Shutterstock pp.21 (potter's wheel/Thirteen), 28 (miscellaneous fruits/Geanina
Bechea), 28 (violin/Nata-Lia), 34 (Jane McIlroy), 39 (urban park/Topanga),
57 (lighthouse/Pawel Kazmierczak), (log cabin/Paul Tessier), 58 (snake/Jay
Ondreicka), 59 (school closed/Africa Studio).